In Sickness and In Silence

*The Trials and Triumphs of
My First Year as a Recovering Addict's Mom*

Kirsten E. Vogel

DEFEAT THE DRAMA
PUBLICATIONS

Troy, MI

In Sickness and In Silence: The Trials and Triumphs of My First Year as a Recovering Addict's Mom

All Rights Reserved

Copyright ©Defeat the Drama Publishing 2018

DEFEAT THE DRAMA
PUBLICATIONS

Defeat the Drama™ is a Registered Trademark
Cover Photos © 2018 Ervin-Edward/Shutterstock.com.

This book is not a medical or mental health manual. The author is not licensed as an educational consultant, teacher, psychologist, counselor, psychiatrist, or medical professional. In the case of a need for any such expertise consult with the appropriate professional. This book details the author's personal experiences and lessons learned from her own life. Recollections of events and opinions about what experiences meant are based on the author's own recall, perceptions and interpretations of those experiences.

Every effort has been made to make this book as accurate as possible. However, there may be typographical and or content errors. Information in this book is intended only to educate and entertain. The author and publisher shall have no liability or responsibility to any person or entity regarding any loss or damage incurred, or alleged to have incurred, directly or indirectly, by the information contained in this book. You hereby agree to be bound by this disclaimer or you may return this book within the guarantee time period for a full refund (thirty days).

This book may not be reproduced, transmitted, or stored in whole or in part by any means, including graphic, electronic, or mechanical without the express written consent of the publisher except in the case of brief quotations embodied in critical articles and reviews.

ISBN 978-0692058190

PRINTED IN THE UNITED STATES OF AMER

Table of Contents

Introduction 1

The Trials And Triumphs Of My First Year As A Recovering Addict's Mom 5

Some Lessons Learned So Far 35

    No One Chooses to Be an Addict 35

    Addiction Can Happen Quickly! 37

    It Won't Happen to Everyone But it *CAN* Happen to Anyone 38

    Create a Foundation of Trust with Your Kids 39

    Avoid the Comfort of Denial - Listen to Your Gut 40

    Release Control, Assess the Situation, Design Support.....Repeat 42

    Strategies to Live Without Guilt 46

    Find Support for Yourself 47

    There Really is No "They" 48

    Loving an Addict is Isolating 53

    The Lesson I *HOPE* to Learn 54

Epilogue 55

Acknowledgements 57

Resources 59

Contact Kirsten 60

Introduction

My son suggested that I start speaking and writing about our story to help others. I guess he's wired like me……channel your challenges into service & support. So, with my son's permission, I am sharing some details from this last year.

I am the mom of a drug addict, who, thankfully, is one year into recovery.

I didn't see it coming. Would never have anticipated this. I think that's probably what most, if not all, who know our family would say as well. It's also probably what many who love an addict say. But, it's true. I'm not sure it's fully sunken in for me. Your mind can only recalibrate so quickly and this past year has required plenty of that. And……this disease has a stigma that keeps you silent….and isolated, turning mostly inward and to God. Even our very closest

Introduction

family and friends have known only some details. So, I haven't spoken out loud about it much.

I've always been a positive, high energy person, who has encouraged others and shared advice. I've even made a profession out of it as a speaker, author, and coach. I've designed a life around looking for the silver lining, fully aware that my reaction to life is what is in my control, and that positive and grateful is the way to be. I have a history of overcoming adversity while remaining positive and focused in the process. This last year, however, has taxed my ability to rally to that level. There are steeper mountains, and this one has been mine. The uphill battle of maneuvering this life while *portraying* an energetic, positive, supportive human, speaker and coach, rather than just *being* one, has been daunting in this circumstance, and I'm certain I've been unsuccessful. The current state of the business I've had for eleven years stands as proof.

While my son wanted me to begin sharing with and encouraging others, it was not my story to tell until he was ready. I admit that, as I release this into the world,

I worry about how some will react. I am bracing for some negative backlash. However, I also look forward, with great anticipation, to the act of liberating what's been bottled up inside for more than a year. I also hope to help others and change perceptions for a few along the way.

And, I know there are people who are in this world too, who have been isolated like me. My hope is that you will read this and know you are in a larger community than you realized and will feel less alone.

I've heard it said that by telling your story first you give others the gift of telling theirs second. Perhaps, my son and I can inspire others to share their stories too, and we can begin to remove the stigma that shouldn't belong to this terrible disease. Yes, it's great to share with others in a similar circumstance but, wow, would it be wonderful to be free and open, to have this be a socially acceptable malady that would allow us to garner the support and compassion of a full community. I have used so much energy hiding what has been our most significant challenge.

Introduction

The brunt of this entire experience, of course, has fallen on my son. He must deal with the consequences of this disease for a lifetime. I am telling this story through my eyes and experience because that is what I know. And, he has asked me to do so in hopes that it can help others. In no way is my sharing meant to minimize or overshadow what he has been through. Perhaps he will soon share what it has felt like for him. In the meantime, I'm not an expert, I'm just a mom. This is my experience and some of what has helped me.

The Trials And Triumphs Of My First Year As A Recovering Addict's Mom

I picked him up from college on December 15th, 2016 as a seemingly successful freshman and exactly one week later, on December 22nd, I was checking my drug addicted son into rehab. Talk about recalibrating your entire life view as you knew it at the speed of *WHOA*!

It has been the most devastating, scary, sad, heart wrenching, overwhelming, anxiety-inducing, shocking, isolating time of my life. I honestly can't even find enough words to stack on top of one another to fully capture how it has felt.

Have you ever hit a patch of black ice while driving with your family on a sunny day? No signs of danger, yet everything changes in a blink. You feel an adrenaline rush as your car moves at its original pace, but is no longer in your control. Your palms sweat and heart races. You wish you could see into the future to know everyone will be fine, but you can't. There are unanticipated twists and turns and potential calamities every second of the wild ride. How could this be? Doesn't the sun guarantee a safe drive? Time slows and your focus narrows to take in every little detail as your brain clicks through possible responses to each iteration. All you can really do, though, is ride it out and hope for the best, while you shout out expletives and quick prayers.

And, when that crazy part of the ride is over, you breathe a sigh of relief, two shaking, sweaty hands at 10:00 and 2:00, held a little tighter on the wheel, with your heart pounding so hard you feel it in your ears. You move on with intense focus, hopeful for a smooth ride, but less certain about what the next mile will bring.

Well, that pretty much sums up how it's felt for the past year. That's 525,600 minutes of unanticipated slick crazy patches that felt completely out of control, followed by calmer moments of gratitude with a dose

In Sickness and In Silence

of hypervigilance and uncertainty about what may come next. 525,600 minutes of peaks and valleys, highs and lows. Moments of heartache and fear, but countless moments of pride too.

Nothing about our son or his life predicted this outcome. Trust me, I've looked! He was always a good child. He followed the rules and was happy and empathetic. He barely cried as a baby, had fewer temper tantrums than most toddlers, and he rarely did anything that required consequences from me as he got older.

He is very intelligent. He said his first words when he was just 8 months old, calling "kee kee" for kitty and "gog gog" for dog, as he crawled to catch our pets. And I still remember our Pediatrician laughing and marveling at how, at 9 months, he seemed to furrow his brow and focus to listen intently during his well visits. We could have really cool conversations by the time he was two. He was reading before he hit school, had decided he'd like to be a paleontologist, and could tell you all about photosynthesis.

As a kindergartner he said, "Mom, I just don't feel like the math is challenging enough for me." By second grade there was talk of moving him up a grade. Middle school and high school went well too. He got good grades with little effort. As a freshman, he was accepted into the School of Performing Arts, was cast in a lot of great roles, and won acting awards all four years. During his senior year he earned more scholarships for his acting skill than any other student in the state. He was recruited like a rock star that fall and his classmates voted him "Most Likely to be Famous."

His own description of himself, shared with his class as a kindergartener, sums him up quite well, "I'm a little bit bad, but mostly good, and I have really good manners."

When his stepdad and I dropped our son off for his first semester of college in August of 2016, we felt like he was really ready to launch. He seemed rock solid, ready for new adventures, confident. He was intelligent, articulate, independent and talented. He had spent years on stage by this point and was always quick with a joke to make others laugh. He had been managing his own schedule and life for years, had earned multiple scholarships to a Big Ten University, and had the grades to get there.

During that first semester, I went to see him quite a few times. I have to admit, I'd use about any excuse to visit him. "Oh, you need new pants? I'll come up and take you shopping!" He seemed mostly good, always delivering news of recent successes. Some of what he shared made it clear he had some more adjusting to do. "I'm not really fitting in." "It's been a little hard to make friends." "I feel small." "Our freshman theatre class isn't really jelling."

I was a little surprised that he was having difficulty, but I wasn't concerned. It was exactly what they told us to anticipate during the parent orientation. I assumed that, if they prepped us for this at orientation, plenty of freshman must be going through the same thing. I thought it was all part of a normal transition from high school to college and he'd work it out. Still, nothing foreshadowed what was to come.

On December 15th, as I drove him home for break, he shared his excitement for the future. Indications were good that college life was moving in the right direction. That first semester had brought lots to celebrate. He was cast in a play and would be traveling to Dubai to perform. He had written a lot of the annual Freshman Showcase, an absurdist humor show, and had acted and directed in it too. His grades were good. The Head of Acting, identifying a lot of talent, was working with him individually, and a jury of 11 theatre professors had given him raving feedback during his semi-annual review.

But…..when we got home…. something wasn't right……he was being secretive, closing his bedroom door, taking a big bag with him everywhere he went. His memory seemed off and he was falling asleep at odd times and places…..he just wasn't……him.

In just that first week we found curious things in his room like a cut straw and empty prescription bottles, saw him falling asleep during a funeral and at the dinner table, noticed slurred speech and forgetfulness, as he got up to take a second shower just 2 hours after the first. Then there was the trip to the ER, a positive drug test and a night following him through the house as he wandered and paced until dawn. It became abundantly clear very quickly that we had a problem that required intervention. This was beyond the scope of my ability as a mom.

Shock can be a wonderful life-saving antidote to adjustment overload. It certainly provided some protection for me that week. My brain couldn't possibly keep up with this swift transition in circumstance. I just needed to stay mentally intact enough to do what needed to be done and, more importantly, be there for my son. No time to slow down and process. I also had to work to keep denial at bay. I really wanted to excuse away the odd findings and behaviors. Too much thinking and I might have slowed our response.

Instead, I worked at a fever's pitch through all of the logistics that had to be worked out on the fly: Where would we take him? What are the steps to admitting him? Would insurance cover anything or would we pay out of pocket? How long would he be there? What would he take with him? What did we need to do to ready our house for his return? What must we do to keep him safe until we leave?

My brain also swirled through a bombardment of culminating questions: How bad is he really? How could he function in school and come home this out of control? Was he this bad at school? For how long? Did others know? What has he been doing? What drugs? How did he get them? How could he function? Is he an addict? What defines an addict? Was his life ever in danger? How did he get so out of control so quickly? How did we get here? Could I have done anything to prevent this? Did I miss clues? What happened? What *WILL* happen? Will he be able to go back to school? What steps will he need to take? Does he really want to get well? And, of course..... *Will he be ok??!??*

In Sickness and In Silence

The torrent of unknowns and an uncertain future created unbearable suspense. If I'd been reading a story I would have flipped to the end to see how it all turned out. But, I was living this out in real time and had to ride it out as it unfolded, second by unending second.

We learned that he needed to make the call to request help. He had just turned 18 and, according to law, some magical transformation happens the moment they hit that milestone. Thankfully, my newly adult son, through his fog, immediately asked, "What do I need to do to go?" His stepdad and I sat with him while he made the call and assisted while he responded to the required questions. Some of his answers unveiled more shocking details. These, too, I tucked away for later. We scheduled a check-in time for later that day and had just a few hours to pack up what he needed and could bring. There were many rules to follow.

We shed tears together as we packed. This was so not the semester break either of us had anticipated. Should he bring a notebook for journaling? Was it ok to bring a pen? Maybe a pencil would be better. What about his Bible? Should he honor the Christmas Eve pajama tradition I'd started when he was a baby or wait to wear them when he was back home at a date yet unknown? We grabbed what we thought he'd need from the clothes he'd just brought home from school to fill a small suitcase.

And then it was time…..to bring his packed suitcase to the car, and drive the hour to the hospital…..where I would say bye to him in the lobby…..and watch him wheel his few belongings through the door that locked behind him. I watched through the tiny window as long as I could and then pried myself away to collapse into my husband's arms…..my rock…..My son was in a safe place in the care of professionals now. Strong mom could let go and take some time to feel the agony of this crisis.

I called my cousin during the ride home. I sobbed as I talked to her and felt hurt and helpless, yet numb, all at the same time. I couldn't even process my own words.

In Sickness and In Silence

My ears heard as if another mouth spoke, as miraculous shock worked to cushion me from the full brunt of this experience. I know there was also a call to my dad to update him and cancel the trip we'd planned to see him for Christmas. I honestly can't remember exactly when it happened or what the full conversation was. A lot of the rest of that day and the next are just a foggy blur.

His third night there fell on Christmas Eve and was one of the worst nights of my life. Have you ever cried so hard that you aren't sure you'll be able to take your next breath? My eyes were almost swollen shut. My nose was so plugged that my ears clicked every time I swallowed and my throat was raw from wailing, as the tears flowed. I dug around for the silver lining, as I always do, and was grateful that he had accepted the help and was in a safe place. But, I could not quiet my mind and heart enough to find any amount of peace. How would I ever sleep? My son should be in his bed across the hall from me sleeping his way towards a family Christmas. Instead, he was in a rehab and I didn't know how he was or what he was doing. I had to release full control to a team of professionals who were strangers to me.

My baby boy. My little Tinka-tink. My world. My pride. My focus for years. My talented, compassionate, and intelligent son, who has in him what it takes to be a gift to the world. How could this be? How would I survive the next few days as the minutes clicked by, each like a separate eternity?

When our kids are young, a simple kiss to a boo boo can heal a hurt in a heartbeat. My baby boy was in pain but there was nothing I could do to take any of it away. I couldn't talk to him or see him for the next few days. Was he ok? How was he feeling? Was he sad or scared? Were they treating him well? Was he having withdrawals? What did his room look like? Did he have a roommate? Who else was in there with him and what were they like? Would he beat this? Would his desire to get well continue as the fog wore off? What would his future bring? When would he get out? What would he be like then? What can we do to support him

In Sickness and In Silence

when he gets out? What do we need to do in our home to prepare? And still......*Will he be ok?*

I did manage to capture a few hours of restless sleep that night. But, as the respite of my slumber faded, I woke to what I wished was a nightmare. The feeling of dread washed over me anew as I forced myself to breathe in and then out. I longed to find sleep again so that more minutes could pass without this misery. Instead, I struggled to focus on the here and now to keep the panic at bay. There was work to do that could occupy my mind.

We spent Christmas morning getting our house ready for my son's return. I knew we needed to create a safe place for him to heal. We were still just guessing about what would be helpful for him. What did we need to lock up or get rid of? Was mouthwash okay? What about aerosol cans or cleaning supplies? I knew little about this world in general and almost nothing about my son and his specific circumstance. I had no idea what would be a trigger for him. I was grateful for Google as a resource that day. We decided to err on

First Year as a Recovering Addict's Mom

the side of caution and just lock it all up. Then it was off to an extended family gathering where I tried to act festive while we shared only that he was sick and couldn't attend.

I drove to pick him up by myself when he was released. We were both nervous. I can't remember a time when the future has felt so uncertain. I didn't know how committed he'd be and he was anxious to learn whether I was mad, disappointed, or supportive. He shook from head to toe as I hugged him. I quickly assured him that I was so proud of him and was there for him as a support system. Our house had been transformed into a safe haven for him and we were ready to take it one step at a time with him.

The many questions that had flooded my brain and fired my curiosity pushed to the forefront. I was eager to ask them all, but knew I had to pace myself. I didn't want our first moments together to feel like an inquisition. I did ask some and he answered most. Even as I write this a year later, however, there are questions I haven't shared. I've since learned that I

In Sickness and In Silence

may never know. It's sometimes better to focus forward than to dive into the details of a past that may be too difficult to hear.

I took him to see our good friends that night, our chosen family. I knew he needed to be loved on and encouraged. They greeted him with hugs and tears and expressions of pride, as they warmed wonderful home cooked food for him. It was exactly what he needed for this time of transition back into the real world.

While we were hopeful that he'd be well enough to go back to school for spring semester, it quickly became clear that the best choice was for him to take time off to heal, learn, and focus on his recovery. It was yet another "things are worse than we thought" moment. The plans for that next semester would not happen. No more exciting trip to Dubai to perform, no more interesting classes, no time with friends. His full focus would be devoted to learning to live with this disease and finding health.

Another tearful chore lay ahead for us; packing up his belongings and bringing them home from his dorm room at school. As we drove there, he shared how sad he was. I told him I was sad too and asked if it was okay if I cried a little bit. We arrived in his dorm room with a role of large black garbage bags, empty suitcases and laundry baskets; all the tools we needed for as swift an exit as possible.

The state of his room told a story of how chaotic his life had become that semester. He'd met me in the lobby or at my car during my last few visits. I had assumed it was for my convenience. Now I knew the truth. I mentally brushed all of that aside as we collected his things, cleaning and throwing away empty liquor bottles and paraphernalia as we worked. Inside, though, it was yet another moment of, "Oh Wow! I can't believe it! This is worse than I realized!" Another circumstance I tucked away for processing at a later date when I was afforded the time. For now, I would focus on the task at a hand and the future.

The next several months brought an abundance of meetings, appointments and outpatient care, requiring several activities each day. It was a full-time job and then some just getting him to where he needed to be. It was exhausting and I was only playing the role of chauffer, he was doing the real work. And, I, on the sidelines of my son's important journey, could do no more to help him than provide a haven for healing and logistical support. I yearned to do more to make the burden of recovery easier.

There was slow but steady progress, ups and downs, celebrating milestones, providing support and encouragement, and many jolting moments as we discovered the impact his mind and body had amassed. Evidence of the damage was worse than I had anticipated and lingered far longer than I had expected. He continued to have night sweats for months and had no appetite. His brain was foggy and his thinking off. Even simple tasks were overwhelming. He slept and slept but was constantly exhausted. There were also revelations about the state of his mental health creating cause for concern. Was it part of recovery or an underlying issue? Only time would tell.

First Year as a Recovering Addict's Mom

There's no roadmap or manual to help with the deluge of new challenges and experiences, no FAQ to consult for answers, and no crystal ball to provide a view into the future. Nothing is black and white, yes or no. I did what I could to gather information quickly. I plugged into some parent support groups, driving an hour each way to find what I needed, and researched and read. I needed to learn how to support him without taking over his recovery, how to parent in a new way, how to recalibrate my life view and my expectations, how to find a sense of calm in this circumstance, and how to move on with at least some small semblance of normalcy. We had redone a bathroom just before the holidays and I'd hung a new picture on the wall that read, "Faith is the light that guides us through the dark storm." Every day I read it and marveled at how soon after purchase these words of wisdom had become so relevant in my life. I'd find comfort in that truth, but wished it had remained a more abstract inspiration.

Meanwhile, new normal had me recalibrating expectations to celebrate that he was clean and going to his meetings, and nothing more. He had been so enthusiastic about life and now did nothing more than the minimum. Should I urge or demand that he get up and do something productive, or is it okay if he sleeps all day? Did I need to wait for him to feel motivated, or should I ignite some action by requiring it? What should I do for him and what should I let go? What was he capable of now? I wanted to find that perfect balance of encouraging him without adding undo pressure that might have him backsliding. It was so hard to know what was right, and so contrary to how I had parented before.

All the while, I was battling against denial. It crept in constantly with promises of comfort in this storm and had me double checking my conclusions non-stop. Was I excusing anything away, allowing for anything I shouldn't, missing any important clues?

I also struggled to define my boundaries. What should I tolerate and what were my wants, needs and desires? How many people from meetings can ride in our car with him, how far and how often? Who do we allow in our house and what are the rules? Do I allow him to hang with a 19-year-old girl, the first person even close to his age that he'd met? She was still using, but planning to get help, and he wanted to encourage her. Do I trust his judgment and ability to set boundaries with her? Do I allow her in my home? His recovery had opened the door to a new world of people with whom he wanted to spend time, creating a plethora of new experiences and parental question marks.

The leader of the parent support group told me, "Just pay attention to what feels right to you", but I needed help developing a new perspective. One moment my son was a college freshman hanging out with 18 year olds at a Big Ten University and the next he was spending time at Narcotics Anonymous meetings with 35 to 70-year-old drug addicts, many of whom had spent time in prison. Some still had no job or driver's license. Logically, I knew that these meetings were what was best and celebrated his commitment to them, but my mom brain still screamed against all of it. I needed help creating a tolerance for this new normal and a new definition of right.

While the weight of each next decision felt immense, my uncertainty blossomed. Weighing the pros and cons of every action and word was exhausting. I'd make a decision only to find myself questioning the last while moving on to the next. Rightly or wrongly, it felt like I needed to do or say just the right thing, but I was never certain what that right thing was. I yearned for a committee to consult to help me with daily choices. Better yet, how wonderful it would be to sit on the sidelines of this life for a breather, to watch with detachment and judge with the advantage of distance and hindsight, rather than feel the enormous weight of responsibility as each moment unfolded.

I couldn't allow the situation to consume me, but pulling away was like battling quicksand. The niggling worry that kept a portion of my mind distracted with thoughts of him and antsy to see him or hear his voice no matter where I was. I wanted, no needed, constant assurance that all was still ok. In those early months, I feared leaving him alone at all. Then it was the concern over the renewed freedom access to the car brought. Once he had a job and money, that new independence sparked the next set of fear. And, when he went back to college, moving from our safe haven straight back into the world of free rein, I white knuckled it some more.

I couldn't generate normalcy for me without concern for my son. And now I think I've learned that really never was the goal. Instead, it seems, it's to live life despite the worry and concern. It's also living with the hard truth that I never really was in charge anyway. My actions, my attentiveness, my hypervigilance were not the variables that would dictate any outcome. Instead, it was his choices, his desires, his work. I had to release control where I never had it to begin with again.....and again.....and again.

And there was the new odd and uncomfortable sensation of keeping the most significant thing happening in my life a secret.....It was consuming me and changing who I was, yet I could not share.

- Spending Christmas morning readying our home for his return and then whisking to a family gathering where we could only say my son was sick and unable to come. Somewhat true, but certainly not the full picture.

- The many nights I found a spot to work nearby as he participated in his Intensive Outpatient Program, trying hard to look normal while I attempted to focus on my screen.

- The business lunches where I skimmed over answers to the simple questions about my family and quietly brushed away tears as the heartache of our circumstance leaked from my eyes.

- Teaching a weekly night class at Oakland University in front of students my son's age and knowing he should be in school too, but wasn't. Acting like a regular professor to focus on the business topics of the class over important life lessons I could have shared.

- Leaving a large business event to take an emergency after-hours call from a doctor, then walking back in with a smile.

- The days I met with clients and acted upbeat and enthusiastic for the day while he received additional intensive care.

- Taking the call from his counselor as I drove to a business lunch to learn that the state of his mental health, the underlying challenge that had him self-medicating in the first place, was beyond her scope. He needed inpatient care and a new counsellor with different skills. Hit, once again, with, "This is worse than we thought" and even more logistics to work out. A quick call to my husband to ask for his help, a swipe at the tears, a glance in the mirror, and then I was shoving all of it aside to tackle this lunch with a smile and an act.

If it had been a broken leg or a socially acceptable illness I'd have shared. Instead, in all of these

In Sickness and In Silence

circumstances and more, I'd hide my hurts and move on like all was well in my world.

So, it's been a year of feeling fake out of necessity, of living with the discomfort of a gaping dichotomy between what I portrayed to the world versus what was truly going on in my life.

A year of bristling inside as someone asked how my kids were doing, unaware of the internal struggle that seemingly simple question ignited. The energy wasted to hide, stuff down, keep secret something I knew should not be shameful but is.

A year of meeting new people and resigning myself to giving them nothing more than broken-but-faking-it me, the best that I could muster.

Months of battling the exhaustion ignited from a life of uncertainty, logistical challenges, and the mental gymnastics required to focus where I was rather than on the worry that consumed me from home.

The heartache of watching others benefit from community support for more "socially acceptable" hardships, while we moved through daunting emotional, financial and logistical challenges isolated, invisible and unable to openly share.

And also, the inability to share our victories, which, absent the back story of our circumstance, would seem less than noteworthy, if not odd; he only woke up in cold sweats twice last night; today he took a shower and ate some food. And, no accolades or recognition for me either for achieving what was huge in my circumstance; just getting up, getting ready, and getting out to create a bit of normal.

So…..this last year has been a roller coaster of crazy twists and turns, of fear and heartache and rejoicing over the small but now significant-in-our-circumstance triumphs. It was a year that moved so fast and furious I rarely had time to slow long enough to think, feel or process. But, while last year's Christmas Eve was the worst of my life, from where I sit today, I believe I was actually receiving a wonderful gift.

I am supremely aware that this is still early recovery and that this disease lasts a lifetime. This is a journey still unfolding, but I do know that, so far, we are all heading hard in the right direction. We have much for which to be grateful. It was difficult having no time to plan for rehab, but I'd take that over the long drawn out fight that many have getting their loved ones to agree to treatment. I'm so grateful he was ready to get well before he endured brushes with the law and even more significant health and life consequences. I'm so relieved that he was ready and pray he stays committed!

I'm grateful for the time I invested in Al-Anon way back in my twenties. It helped me end and move on from a partnership then and has provided a base of knowledge I can use for a relationship I'll *never* give up on now. I'm thankful that we picked up on small clues that telegraphed trouble, did our due diligence, and moved past denial to take action quickly. I'm thankful that my marriage has stood with a solid foundation of love and commitment through the hardships of heartache, uncertainty, and logistical and financial upheaval. I'm grateful for the few family and friends who checked on us periodically and kept us in their prayers. We have faith in a God who holds us up through tough times and will channel this challenge into something positive! I am sure of this and wait, willingly and with as much patience as I can find.

And, there have been so many moments of pride. I'm proud of the tenacity with which he has attacked his recovery. He started going to NA and AA meetings the day after he got out of rehab, going daily at least once, and often more. And he continued to get outpatient care.

He has had tough conversations with people he admires, owning up to his choices and circumstance. His trip to meet with the Head of Acting face to face definitely stands out as extraordinary. He chose to look him in the eye rather than email or text to deliver the tough news that he would not be returning to school or playing the large role in the performance scheduled in Dubai. Courageous and so helpful to his recovery!

He has grown leaps and bounds. As a teen, he has already learned and implemented many great life strategies that have him surpassing clients I've worked with who still struggled in their 50's. He has learned to identify his needs and communicate them. He is not embarrassed by his illness and shares his story to encourage others and to create accountability around himself.

He has learned to watch for triggers and stay off a road that leads back to use. He is tapping into the resources he must to stay on the path to health. Those he's met in recovery have all been significantly older than him but that hasn't stopped him. He's embraced the new relationships and learned from those who go before him on this journey.

And, more amazing, he's back in school in an environment not easily conducive to staying clean. He has jumped back in to real world *PLUS* and has managed a full class load, work, meetings, and Doctor's appointments back home, all while maintaining good grades. He is appreciating and using his recaptured free time to do what he loves; joining a university improvisation troupe, doing stand-up comedy at open mic nights, and acting in whatever film or play comes his way.

As I look towards a new year with hope and enthusiasm, my prayer is that we find a little time to reflect and process. I'd like to celebrate what we've been through and the progress that we've made, while we continue to forward our growth. I pray that we find opportunities to help others through what we've learned. Please God, let me, once again, use my gifts to serve others.....I've so missed living out my purpose.

Some Lessons Learned So Far

∽

I am certainly *NOT* an expert. However, I have learned some things that may help others. They may be very elementary or not even 100% accurate but, with these disclaimers, here are some of my lessons learned, new perspectives and strategies. They have helped me.

No One Chooses to Be an Addict

I've had people ask me how I can deal with the anger I must feel towards my son. The thing is, I have felt sad, terrified, shocked, confused, heartbroken, compassionate, uncertain, isolated. One thing I have not been is angry. My son is sick. Did he make some bad choices? Absolutely. But they were choices that many college students make, the same choices many of us older people made at that time in our lives, or are still making. And, how many of us know people who self-medicate to cover up hurts? So, while I don't excuse away his bad choices, he must own those, the unanticipated outcome of those choices is not his doing. He experienced this outcome because his body was predisposed to react to chemicals differently than most. No one can know whether they have the gene until it's too late. So, while he certainly chose to use what he used, he did *NOT* choose to have the reaction he had.

I don't know of one person on this earth who picked up a first beer, smoked marijuana or took their prescribed pain or anti-anxiety meds and said, "I can't wait to be an addict!" No, no one sees around that corner to predict a life that is out of control. Taking the substance starts you on a path with an unknown destination. And no one would choose the one of addiction. No, the path to addiction begins with some seemingly harmless choices that divert some down a path no one envisions. Anyone using any kind of substance, whether for fun, for medical reasons, or to fill a hole in the soul, is rolling the dice.

Addiction Can Happen Quickly!

It was beyond my comprehension how he could go from functioning teen to drug addict in a matter of months. This illustration that I learned in the parent support group has helped me understand how this is possible. Visualize that everyone is born with a sponge in their brain. Everyone's sponge is a different size, some very small, some medium, and some large. Once that sponge is saturated, a person is an addict. Some people can drink and drug for years without losing control. Some abuse and then back off. They may suffer legal or relationship consequences but are able to take a break or slow down. Others become addicted very quickly and are soon out of control. If a person introduces chemicals at a young age the size of their sponge can become smaller. In my son's case, it didn't take much for him to become addicted. His illustrative sponge is obviously quite small.

It Won't Happen to Everyone But it *CAN* Happen to Anyone

This disease doesn't discriminate. It appears along the lines of any race, economic status, level of education, or geography, and isn't limited to a specific kind of upbringing. The only distinguishing factor I have learned is probably the opposite of what most would assume. According to what some professionals have shared with me, in general, addicts have higher than normal intelligence.

My son does come from a "broken home" and he is intelligent, but nothing foreshadowed this outcome to me. As I've already described, he was a really good child. Always respectful, communicative, funny and easy going.

And, I'm sure there's no such thing as a perfect parent, but I do know I was a good mom. I made my kids a priority and tried to minimize my mistakes. I read to them when they were little, did homework with them when they started school, and was at all of their games and events. I was one of the stricter parents, waiting longer to allow them to go to movies or the mall. We spent tons of time in Northern Michigan with my family swimming, fishing, roasting marshmallows over a campfire. Lots of good wholesome fun. And, my kids grew up in church, actively volunteering for years.

And, yet, here we are.

Create a Foundation of Trust with Your Kids

Build trust while your kids are young so that if life goes awry you'll have the foundation of that relationship. Our strong bond couldn't fully cushion him from life challenges and doesn't guarantee the outcome we've experienced thus far, but, I thank GOD for all the time I poured into my kids over the years. I guarantee I wasn't perfect, but when my son needed rehab, he trusted me. Yes, he had to be ready! It was his recovery, but his trust allowed him to take the support I was suggesting. Thank God, we didn't have to maneuver through the muck of a dysfunctional relationship during this time of crisis.

Avoid the Comfort of Denial - Listen to Your Gut

Our initial clues to this new circumstance were subtle, taken individually. I could easily have silenced what I feared by focusing instead on my false beliefs. Your mind can play tricks and excuse away facts. I admit I did wrestle with some of these thoughts for a bit:

- He was overly tired and forgetting a lot, but this could just be the repercussions from a tough finals week.

- He was closing his bedroom door and carrying a large bag with him wherever he went, but maybe this was just a new habit created while living in a college dorm.

- Empty prescription bottles could mean he was sick and didn't tell me, or someone gave him prescription allergy medicine to use in place of the over the counter stuff he sometimes used.

- An empty pen casing could have just fallen apart in his bag and a cut straw might have been part of a game.

- Falling asleep in his dinner and then having a positive drug test in the ER could just mean he's new to experimenting with drugs and doesn't know how to handle them well.

- His upbringing doesn't suggest he could end up with a drug problem.

- His grades in college were good and all of his successes stand as evidence that he is fine.

There is comfort in believing the best in the face of evidence that suggests otherwise, but this can leave you enabling the sick behavior longer than you should. My brain wanted to deny the possibility of a drug problem and excuse away what we found, but my mom gut was spot on.

Each separate curious behavior or finding might have proved innocent on its own, but combining all that we saw painted the full picture. Within days we were acting to solve a problem I still did not *WANT* to believe in, and knew little about. There was much uncertainty, but my actions still moved us in one specific direction; trying to avoid anything that helped him continue the destructive behavior, choosing, instead, to harness my full focus toward actions that would support his health. Period.

Release Control, Assess the Situation, Design Support.....Repeat

What I have found is that, for me, loving an addict means constantly going against what my initial instincts are. Watching him struggle ignited my desire to jump in and take all the work away from him. And I wanted to dictate his every move like I somehow had the magic formula. It was not natural for me to break away to move on with my own life. I knew I had to and I did, but my mind stayed distracted and attached to my son and this disease that I could not control. I've had to be very intentional with my actions and words.

I simplified the guidelines I made for myself:

- Don't do too much. He must make choices and take action.
- Don't do too little. Lighten his load. Support can show love and acceptance.
- All actions must support movement towards health.
- I still need a life too.

The problem, of course, is that it is very difficult to define "too little" and "too much" and swiftly shifting circumstances can change these targets constantly.

It's his recovery. I can't do this for him. I can't remove the pain. Instead, I do my best to find the right balance between supporting him in his recovery without taking it over; allowing him to be responsible without setting the expectations unreasonably high; and helping him where I can without coddling him or enabling bad behavior.

I found myself assessing constantly. As I said earlier, rightly or wrongly, it felt like I needed to do or say just

Some Lessons Learned So Far

the right thing, but I was never certain what that right thing was. It was already a time of transition in our relationship. When he went away to college there was a shift in our roles as he became more independent. I had stepped back to leave more decisions and actions to his control. Bringing him home as a drug addict required a more precarious balancing dance with a much swifter tempo.

My goal is to support him in his recovery without making decisions for him or enabling any behavior that keeps him stuck in his illness. Period. I've had to examine every action and constantly shift my support to make it reasonable for the current circumstance:

- Should I help him find NA meetings? At the beginning of his recovery, while his brain was extra foggy, yes! I would help a relative find physical therapy resources after surgery so why wouldn't I help my son with this? If I had still been searching for meetings 6 months in, that would be a different story.

- Should I drive him to meetings? In our circumstance, again, it's a yes for the first month after rehab. We didn't allow him to drive our car and he didn't want that responsibility yet. I was able to drive him and did. Over time, as he got better and continued on his positive path, he asked for more freedom and we gave it.

- Should I help him enroll in his classes as he returned to school? Answer, this is moving him forward not helping him stay stuck and is something I might do even if he wasn't sick so, yes. I'll be there as a sounding board and will help him maneuver through the schedule builder. He calls the shots, but I help with the logistics.

It's required constant evaluation as targets of support verses independence move. Over this past year we've had a gradual shift from higher support to higher independence. Each little transformation required analysis, recalibration and intentional action. There is no specific right answer and no manual to peruse. I've learned to do the best I can, giving myself grace, and tweaking where I must along the way.

Strategies to Live Without Guilt

Every unnatural rule or request brought the opportunity for guilt. The sentiment I kept top of mind always was, "I love my son, but I hate the disease. I trust my son, but I don't trust the disease." I stay very clear on this distinction to avoid feeling guilty for the safeguards we put in place. Locking up everything in our house is not distrust of my son, it is distrust of his disease. Creating rules about his room and driving, drug testing when I saw behavior that made me concerned, keeping my purse and money behind a locked door in my room. The safeguards were what helped me feel comfortable and he adhered to willingly but, not going to lie, it still felt odd.

Find Support for Yourself

If you love an addict, it is unlikely that he or she will traverse this disease without impacting you and the rest of the family. I'm so grateful for the knowledge I have from my earlier participation in Al-Anon and all of the reading I did on this subject back in my twenties. And, I don't know where I'd be today if I hadn't found the parent support group I attend now. It has been so affirming hearing from other parents. I feel less alone and can learn from others' successes and their missteps too. And, having a professional who also has personal experience in the world of addiction has been invaluable. She's been my sounding board for many crossroads, helped me recalibrate my perspective and define success in new normal. There are also Al-Anon meetings, Nar-Anon, Families Anonymous, counseling and more. Find what works for you and plug in. Do not do this alone!

There Really is No "They"

Before I was in this world, I thought that my family was different from addicts and those who loved them. I think it's what we often assume when something scares us. It's human nature. We look for all the ways that our circumstance is different from what we don't understand. It helps quell the fear that the scary thing might happen to us. We tell ourselves we're different and it won't.

We might even take it a step further by looking for ways our circumstance is not only different but better. From this place of judgement, we might find even more cushion as we look down on those who suffer from what we dread.

But, this disease does not discriminate. Addicts and those who love them are not anomalies. Thus, I hate to break it to you but, any "they" you define is not real and shouldn't offer comfort. I am ashamed to admit that I only know this from my personal experience, not because I squelched the ignorance through study.

In Sickness and In Silence

I have recalibrated my perceptions over the past year, each stripping away another level of my prejudice and transforming my "they." It hasn't happened easily, and I'm quite certain I'm not done.

I drove my son to all of his meetings and appointments for the first month and experienced a round of shock as I sat in the parking lot watching the participants roll in; the clothes, the worn looks, the shallow eyes and skinny bodies. Many in this world have lived hard, hard lives that are still beyond my comprehension. Before some meetings, I'd watch a van pull up to bring an entire group from a halfway house. My mind saw a group of hard core, life knocked them down, tattooed, rough looking people. And behind them, in stark contrast, would walk my 18-year-old son with his flannel shirt, jeans, high top tennis shoes and a backwards hat, looking about as All-American as you can get. He'd approach the group to chat, shake hands and hug some. In my mind I screamed, "He doesn't belong there!!" But I had to shift my thinking. He did and he does. He hasn't lived the tough road that many there have, thankfully, but he shares the same disease.

He met a 19-year-old in a partial hospitalization program. She was the first person his own age he'd talked to in months. She had been kicked out of her mom's house after a days long bender, was living on a friend's couch, and still using. As we stood in my living room, she shared openly about her mental illness and the fact that some guy had stolen her prescribed medicine a few days before. She explained, nonchalantly, that she was manic and would probably get much worse soon. I echoed what her mom had told her, to call a charity that could help replace her medicine. She had the number but just hadn't made the call. I was calm and empathetic. However, on the inside I wrestled with what to do. I had never really anticipated having a conversation like this in my own home. Truth be told, I'd never had a conversation like that anywhere in my entire life.

I wanted to feel like we were different. The reality was, not so much. Obviously, my son shared some similar challenges, or they wouldn't have met in a partial hospitalization program and, he too was an addict. So, there she was, reminding me again, that we had been thrust into this new world and, beneath the disease, she was not really different. I'm sure if I met her mom, I'd find similarities there too. She was likely reeling, just like I would have been, from the tough but necessary choice she'd made to kick her drug addicted daughter out for not following her rules.

In the spring, on a chilly afternoon, we all went to a Tiger Game. We had been gifted the tickets from a great friend who knew we needed some family fun. It was months into his recovery and was the first time that my son was out in the world doing something that wasn't a meeting or a Doctor's appointment. As we approached the stadium, we encountered a man who was passed out on the sidewalk, the obvious effects of too much drugging or drinking. I walked to the other side of the street to avoid him. Nothing in my mind linked anything about that man to my son. That is, until he, with great compassion, checked on the man and then went to alert a police officer to find him some help. That's when it hit me, again, like a ton of bricks. My son is an addict. He has the same disease as that man. I was ashamed of myself and so proud of my son. I was learning from him. That man was not a "they" he was a "we", a human in need.

In the support groups, I began to meet others who loved addicts too. It was immediately clear that there was really no difference between us either. In fact, to look around the room, we could just as easily have been in a PTA meeting, if you overlooked the tear soaked cheeks, boxes of Kleenex and the shocked appearance on the newcomers' faces. Most participants come from "normal" homes, good neighborhoods, some very wealthy, and are educated.

There is no stereotypical addict and no stereotypical addict family member. People impacted by this disease, either directly or through relationship, are just that, people.

Loving an Addict is Isolating

There is a stigma to this disease.
That stigma inspires our silence.
Our silence helps perpetuate the stigma.
It's not our story to tell.
Loving an addict is isolating.

The stats are all over the news, drug addiction is an epidemic. What I hadn't ever stopped to consider, though, is that almost every addict represents a community of people who loves them and whose lives have been impacted by this disease. But, we don't share openly with those outside this world. The anticipated reaction is too uncertain, and it's not our story to tell. There are millions of us with this shared experience, but there are no identifying features as we act our way through each day. So, the stigma keeps us isolated from the world, and even from each other.

For now.....we will feel isolated.

The Lesson I *HOPE* to Learn

As I send this out into the world, I know I run the risk of negative backlash. Maybe we'll lose some we thought were friends. Some strangers may make negative comments. But, after a year of staying silent, my hope is that I learn that there is comfort, freedom, and healing in sharing, for both me and my son.

My wish and prayer is that others in a similar situation can find a few strategies to help, a feeling of belonging and hope, and a comfort in knowing they are not alone.

Perhaps some will find new courage to share their story a little more too, so that the cloud of shame, the stigma that should not be, can begin to lift in a world that can be filled with judgement. In silence, we stand alone with an imagined response. By sharing my hope is that our voices grow louder and that out of the isolation we'll find compassion, understanding and support.

Epilogue

As I said before, I'm not an expert, I'm just a mom. These are our experiences and my feelings and responses to this past year. I don't know whether I've done things well or right. I just share…..to share, and perhaps you will do the same.

It's been just over a year now since my son chose rehab. We celebrated the anniversary by throwing him a small surprise party. It was a gathering of close family members and a few of his college friends. His roommate traveled almost 3 hours to be there. It was a really nice night to show appreciation for his important first step and the great work he's done since.

I feel like I've been smiling and laughing for real for the first time in more than a year and it's felt really nice. His successful transition back to school has helped quiet my worry some and reaching that one year milestone seems significant.

I hesitate to even write about what I fear. I know the statistics and realize that recovery without relapse is rare. And while a year is significant it's also not long. I'm in the aftermath of the black ice part of the ride where you breathe a sigh of relief, two shaking, sweaty hands at 10:00 and 2:00, held a little tighter on the wheel, hopeful for a smooth ride, but uncertain about what the next mile will bring.

Today, he is on a strong path, doing what he needs to do to stay well. And, as the dog tag reads, that I gave him as a gift, "One Year, One Day at a Time." I'll continue to release control where I never really had it. I'll keep hope at the forefront, prayers on my lips, and a fervent love for my son in my heart, always and forever.

Acknowledgements

~

I want to thank Julie B., who runs the parent support group I've been attending. Without her I'm not sure where I'd be. She has the education, but also years of both personal and professional experience in the world of addiction. I am so grateful for her advice, insight and encouragement. She has been my North Star. It was wonderful knowing I could collect my questions and bring them to her and the group on Tuesday nights.

I also thank her for reading the manuscript for this book and encouraging me to share it with others.

Thank you to my husband. I could never say it enough. It's been a rough year. He chose to jump on board as a father to my boys when they were young. We had no idea our journey would take us here. Stepparent is not an easy role under any circumstance and, even in this challenge, he has filled that role with grace. He's the one both boys think of first when there's a flat tire and that says a lot. He has been by my side through all of this with no genetic ties. He has loved them through such tough stuff and has loved me through some of my worst. He is my rock and my biggest encourager and supporter.

And, of course, I want to thank my son. He is amazing and has worked so hard. I love him more than he will ever know. I am so proud of him and, as always, am so lucky to be his mom.

Resources

If you are worried about a family member or friend, I highly recommend finding support for you. This disease impacts everyone! There are so many options. Meetings happen all over and at different times. You can also attend some via phone or online. There are counselors who specialize in addiction and family support groups. Facebook has many different groups that provide online connection as well. The one I attend in person is offered for free through the rehab facility my son used. The list here are the tried and true, around forever, options that are available everywhere. It is very small compared to what you will find once you start looking. Search, give some a try and keep going until you find what works for you.

Al-Anon: Members are people, just like you, who are worried about someone with a drinking problem. Based on the 12 steps. al-anon.org

Nar-Anon: For anyone worried about a family member or friend struggling with substances. Based on the 12 steps. nar-anon.org

Families Anonymous: A 12 Step fellowship for the family and friends of those individuals with drug, alcohol or related behavioral issues.
familiesanonymous.org

Contact Kirsten

Kirsten is available for speaking, interviews, or coaching.
Contact her here:
Email: Info@DefeatTheDrama.com
Phone: 248.973.7595
Website: DefeatTheDrama.com

Made in the USA
Columbia, SC
04 February 2018